How to · Receive Communion

KENNETH COPELAND

KENNETH
COPELAND
PUBLICATIONS

Unless otherwise noted, all scripture is from the *King James Version* of the Bible.

How to Receive Communion

ISBN-10 0-88114-796-6   30-0040

ISBN-13 978-0-88114-796-4

12 11 10 09 08 07   24 23 22 21 20

© 1982 International Church of the Word of Faith Inc. now known as Eagle Mountain International Church Inc. aka Kenneth Copeland Ministries

Kenneth Copeland Publications
Fort Worth, TX 76192-0001

For more information about Kenneth Copeland Ministries, call 800-600-7395 or visit www.kcm.org.

HOW TO Receive Communion

When a believer partakes of the Lord's Supper, he should do so with full understanding of its significance. Communion, to many people, has become only a religious observance. It has a much deeper meaning than that.

The Communion table is an emblem of Jesus' sacrifice for us. *Jesus took bread, and blessed it, and broke it, and said, Take, eat; this is my body. And he took the cup, and gave thanks, and gave it to them saying, Drink ye all of it; For this is my blood of the new testament, which is shed for many for the remission of sins* (Matthew 26:26-28).

Primarily, the Church has centered

its attention on the wine as an emblem of Jesus' blood that was shed for sin. We take the emblem of blood and say, "Thank God, we are delivered from sin," and that is true! Praise God for it! But the blood is only half of Communion. The bread is an emblem of Jesus' body that was broken for us. The emblem for His body is just as important as the emblem for His blood.

According to Isaiah 53:4-5, Jesus' sacrifice covered every area of man's existence. He bore spiritual torment for sins, mental distress for our worry, care and fear as well as physical pain for our sickness and disease. The stripes He bore were for our healing. With His stripes we are healed. **God gave everything He had to redeem mankind from the curse.** For us to receive only part of His sacrifice is an insult to Him.

When we receive Communion, we are

receiving His body and His blood. Every time we partake, we should examine ourselves closely according to 1 Corinthians 11:28-29. *But let a man examine himself, and so let him eat of that bread, and drink of that cup. For he that eateth and drinketh unworthily, eateth and drinketh damnation to himself, not discerning the Lord's body.* There is much more involved in receiving Communion than most Christians realize.

God instituted the Lord's Supper for a reason. When you receive it, you should be ready to partake of everything Jesus' sacrifice provided—salvation, peace of mind, healing, total prosperity. In the past, we have missed the full meaning of Communion by not completely judging ourselves when we partake of it. We have been ready to receive His blood and quick to judge ourselves where sin is concerned. We judge ourselves of sin and repent of it.

But what about His body? It was broken for us. It was bruised for us. The stripes laid on Jesus' back were for our healing. At Communion, we should judge ourselves where sickness is concerned as well. **Jesus purchased our healing at Calvary just as He purchased our salvation.** With this in mind, we say, "Lord, it's not right that I should suffer from sickness and disease. I judge it now as being from Satan, and I reject it. I refuse to receive it any longer. I partake of the sacrifice of Your body, and I receive the healing that You provided in Jesus' Name."

When you partake of Communion, make a point of judging yourself to the fullest extent. Don't just receive it halfway. **Accept everything Jesus' sacrifice provided.** If you don't examine yourself—if you receive Communion just as a religious exercise—you will be eating and drinking unworthily, not discerning the Lord's body. Paul wrote, *For this cause many are weak and sickly among you, and many sleep* (1 Corinthians 11:30).

When the first Passover was instituted, God instructed Moses to kill a lamb, to spread its blood over the door, and then roast the lamb and eat all of it. Any that remained was to be burned away. That sacrificial lamb was completely consumed! Jesus, as the Lamb of God, was the supreme sacrifice under the Abrahamic Covenant. When you partake of His sacrifice, do not take only part of it. Take it all! Consume it completely! When you receive the Lord's Supper, do so like the children of Israel. Exodus 12:11 says: *And thus shall ye eat it; with your loins girded, your shoes on your feet, and your staff in your hand; and ye shall eat it in haste: it is the Lord's passover.* The children of Israel were ready to go. They ate in faith. They were ready to receive their deliverance before they ate!

No matter what you may be faced with—sin, sickness, drugs, a weight problem, worry, strife, old habits—you can be delivered through properly receiving the Lord's Supper. **The body and blood of Jesus covered every area of your existence.** By discerning His body and judging yourself before Him, you can receive your deliverance. **Place yourself before God and receive Communion as the children of Israel did—ready to receive your deliverance!**

You do not have to wait until you go to church to receive Communion. Receive it at home. Get up an hour earlier in the morning every now and then. Take the time to put yourself before God over the Communion table. It will be time well spent. I guarantee it! Praise God!

1 Corinthians 11:23-24; Matthew 26: 26-28; Luke 22:19-20

Proclamation Before the Breaking of the Bread:

"Father God, in the Name of Jesus, we recognize that we have a covenant with You—a covenant that was ratified by the shed blood of Jesus at Calvary.

"Because of the fact that Jesus' body was broken for us, that His blood was shed in our behalf, we acknowledge that He bore sin, sickness, disease, sorrow, grief, fear, torment, unforgiveness, strife and lack for us. Through His substitutionary sacrifice, we have complete redemption, total deliverance from the works of Satan.

"As new creations in Christ Jesus, we realize our freedom has been bought and paid

9

for. We are forgiven. We are redeemed. And we give thanks for it all, in Jesus' Name."

Break the Bread and Distribute It

Judge and Examine Yourselves in the Light of God's Word.

"Father, in the Name of Jesus, we examine our own hearts, we judge ourselves according to the authority of Your Word.

"In areas where we have missed the mark (strife, unforgiveness, jealousy, envy, hatred, covetousness, fear, worry, unbelief, etc.), we take Jesus as our Advocate and High Priest. We ask forgiveness according to the Word of God (1 John 1:9). Your Word says You are faithful and just to forgive us when we confess our sins and to cleanse us from all unrighteousness.

"Therefore, we do not eat of the bread nor drink of the cup unworthily, but we rightly discern the Lord's body. We receive Communion together now as the right-eousness of God in Christ Jesus. We are free from the works of Satan—spirit, soul and body." Then say this: *The Lord Jesus the same night in which he was betrayed took bread: And when he had given thanks, he brake it, and said, Take, eat: this is my body, which is broken for you: this do in remem-brance of me (1 Corinthians 11:23-24).*

Partake of the Bread Together

Then say this: *After the same manner also he took the cup, when he had supped, saying, This cup is the new testament in my blood: this do ye, as oft as ye drink it, in re-membrance of me. For as often as ye eat this bread, and drink this cup, ye do show the Lord's death till he come.*

Partake of the Cup Together

Now Join Hands Together and Make This Confession

"Father, we give You thanks for all You have provided for us in Christ Jesus. We confess this day we are the blessed of the Lord. This covenant we entered into at the new birth is a covenant filled with the exceeding great and precious promises of God, and we are partakers of those promises now!

"We are healed. We are redeemed. We are delivered from the authority of darkness. We are translated into the kingdom of God's dear Son. We are the head and not the tail. We are above and not beneath. We come behind in no good thing. All that we set our hands to prospers, and we praise You, Father, for the newness of life we now enjoy. In Jesus' Name, Amen."

Prayer for Salvation and Baptism in the Holy Spirit

Heavenly Father, I come to You in the Name of Jesus. Your Word says, "Whosoever shall call on the name of the Lord shall be saved" (Acts 2:21). I am calling on You. I pray and ask Jesus to come into my heart and be Lord over my life according to Romans 10:9-10: "If thou shalt confess with thy mouth the Lord Jesus, and shalt believe in thine heart that God hath raised him from the dead, thou shalt be saved. For with the heart man believeth unto righteousness; and with the mouth confession is made unto salvation." I do that now. I confess that Jesus is Lord, and I believe in my heart that God raised Him from the dead.

I am now reborn! I am a Christian—a child of Almighty God! I am saved! You also said in Your Word, "If ye then, being evil, know how to give good gifts unto your children: HOW MUCH MORE shall your heavenly Father give the Holy Spirit to them that ask him?" (Luke 11:13). I'm also asking You to fill me with the Holy Spirit. Holy Spirit, rise up within me as I praise God. I fully expect to speak with other tongues as You give me the utterance (Acts 2:4). In Jesus' Name. Amen!

Begin to praise God for filling you with the Holy Spirit. Speak those words and syllables you receive—not in your own language, but the language given to you by the Holy Spirit. You have to use your own voice. God will not force you to speak. Don't be concerned with how it sounds. It is a heavenly language!

Continue with the blessing God has given you and pray in the spirit every day.

You are a born-again, Spirit-filled believer. You'll never be the same!

Find a good church that boldly preaches God's Word and obeys it. Become a part of a church family who will love and care for you as you love and care for them.

We need to be connected to each other. It increases our strength in God. It's God's plan for us.

Make it a habit to watch the *Believer's Voice of Victory* television broadcast and become a doer of the Word, who is blessed in his doing (James 1:22-25).

About the Author

Kenneth Copeland is co-founder and president of Kenneth Copeland Ministries in Fort Worth, Texas, and best-selling author of books that include *How to Discipline Your Flesh* and *Honor—Walking in Honesty, Truth and Integrity.*

Now in his 40th year as a minister of the gospel of Christ and teacher of God's Word, Kenneth is the recording artist of such award-winning albums as his Grammy-nominated *Only the Redeemed, In His Presence, He Is Jehovah, Just a Closer Walk* and his most recently released *Big Band Gospel* album. He also co-stars as the character Wichita Slim in the children's adventure videos *The Gunslinger, Covenant Rider* and the movie *The Treasure of Eagle Mountain,* and as Daniel Lyon in the *Commander Kellie and the Superkids*₅ₘ videos *Armor of Light* and *Judgment: The Trial of Commander Kellie.*

With the help of offices and staff in the United States, Canada, England, Australia, South Africa and Ukraine, Kenneth is fulfilling his vision to boldly preach the uncompromised Word of God from the top of this world, to the bottom, and all the way around. His ministry reaches millions of people worldwide through daily and Sunday TV broadcasts, magazines, teaching audios and videos, conventions and campaigns, and the World Wide Web.

Learn more about Kenneth Copeland Ministries by visiting our Web site at www.kcm.org

Books Available From Kenneth Copeland Ministries

by Kenneth Copeland

by Gloria Copeland

* Available in Spanish

Pressing In—It's Worth It All
Shine On!
The Grace That Makes Us Holy
The Power to Live a New Life
The Protection of Angels
There Is No High Like the Most High
The Secret Place of God's Protection (gift book with CD enclosed)
The Unbeatable Spirit of Faith
This Same Jesus
To Know Him
True Prosperity
Walk With God
Well Worth the Wait
Words That Heal (gift book with CD enclosed)
Your Promise of Protection—The Power of the 91st Psalm

Books Co-Authored by Kenneth and Gloria Copeland

Family Promises
Healing Promises
Prosperity Promises
Protection Promises

* From Faith to Faith—A Daily Guide to Victory
From Faith to Faith—A Perpetual Calendar

One Word From God Can Change Your Life

One Word From God Series:
- One Word From God Can Change Your Destiny
- One Word From God Can Change Your Family

Other Books Published by KCP

Products Designed for Today's Children and Youth

* Available in Spanish

Baby Praise Christmas Board Book
Noah's Ark Coloring Book
The Best of *Shout!* Adventure Comics
The *Shout!* Giant Flip Coloring Book
The *Shout!* Joke Book
The *Shout!* Super-Activity Book
Wichita Slim's Campfire Stories

***Commander Kellie and the Superkids*_{SM} Books:**

The SWORD Adventure Book
*Commander Kellie and the Superkids*_{SM}
   Solve-It-Yourself Mysteries
*Commander Kellie and the Superkids*_{SM}
   Adventure Series:
   Middle Grade Novels by Christopher P.N. Maselli:

#1 The Mysterious Presence
#2 The Quest for the Second Half
#3 Escape From Jungle Island
#4 In Pursuit of the Enemy
#5 Caged Rivalry
#6 Mystery of the Missing Junk
#7 Out of Breath
#8 The Year Mashela Stole Christmas
#9 False Identity
#10 The Runaway Mission
#11 The Knight-Time Rescue of
     Commander Kellie

World Offices
Kenneth Copeland Ministries

For more information about KCM and a free
catalog, please write the office nearest you:

Kenneth Copeland Ministries
Fort Worth, TX 76192-0001

Kenneth Copeland
Locked Bag 2600
Mansfield Delivery Centre
QUEENSLAND 4122
AUSTRALIA

Kenneth Copeland
Post Office Box 15
BATH
BA1 3XN
U.K.

Kenneth Copeland
Private Bag X 909
FONTAINEBLEAU
2032
REPUBLIC OF
SOUTH AFRICA

Kenneth Copeland
PO Box 3111 STN LCD 1
Langley BC V3A 4R3
CANADA

Kenneth Copeland Ministries
Post Office Box 84
L'VIV 79000
UKRAINE

We're Here for You!

Believer's Voice of Victory Television Broadcast

Join Kenneth and Gloria Copeland and the *Believer's Voice of Victory* broadcasts Monday through Friday and on Sunday each week, and learn how faith in God's Word can take your life from ordinary to extraordinary. This teaching from God's Word is designed to get you where you want to be—*on top!*

You can catch the *Believer's Voice of Victory* broadcast on your local, cable or satellite channels.* Also available 24 hours on webcast at BVOV.TV.

* Check your local listings for times and stations in your area.

Believer's Voice of Victory Magazine

Enjoy inspired teaching and encouragement from Kenneth and Gloria Copeland and guest ministers each month in the *Believer's Voice of Victory* magazine. Also included are real-life testimonies of God's miraculous power and divine intervention in the lives of people just like you!

It's more than just a magazine—it's a ministry.

To receive a FREE subscription to
Believer's Voice of Victory, write to:

Kenneth Copeland Ministries
Fort Worth, TX 76192-0001
Or call:
800-600-7395
(7 a.m.-5 p.m. CT)
Or visit our Web site at:
www.kcm.org

If you are writing from outside the U.S., please contact the KCM office nearest you. Addresses for all Kenneth Copeland Ministries offices are listed on the previous pages.